DR KNIT'S
CURIOUS CREATURES

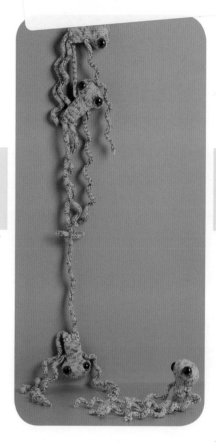

DR KNIT'S
CURIOUS CREATURES

WARM-HEARTED AND WHIMSICAL KNITTED TOY TALES AND PATTERNS

Arturo Azcona

Photography by Jean-Philippe Woodland

Fil Rouge Press

For Ben, who always believed in me

First published in the United Kingdom in 2015 by
Fil Rouge Press, 46 Voss Street, London E2 6HP

ISBN 978-0-9927923-2-9

Printed in Malaysia

A CIP catalogue record for this book is available from the
British Library

10 9 8 7 6 5 4 3 2 1

Publisher: Judith More
Managing Editor: Jennifer Latham
Pattern Editor: Katy Bevan
Designer: Elizabeth Healey
Photographer: Jean-Phillippe Woodland

Fil Rouge Press books are available from all good bookshops.
Alternatively, contact the publisher direct on
www.filrougepress.com

Note: Unless otherwise specified in the Materials lists, you will
not need more than one ball/skein of each of the specified
yarn colours.

WARNING: Do not give these toys to babies or young children.
The curious creatures are art toys. They were not designed for
children as they have small parts and could pose a hazard.

CONTENTS

· · · · · · · · · · · · · · · ·

INTRODUCTION

Dr Knit and his Knitting Laboratory were first created as a series of art exhibitions. People of all ages are entranced by the strange creatures they meet in the Laboratory, all of whom have a problem that Dr Knit resolves for them. Each problem embodies an aspect, or aspects, of a child's experience.

I have always believed that inside all of us there is a childlike side that is ultimately more truthful, honest and open than our adult exterior. I also believe that this is a part of us we don't often allow or let out once we reach adulthood. Through the creatures I create and the stories behind them I invite my readers to relax and let their childlike imagination take hold, connecting with feelings or states they may have lost contact with.

Like medicine or therapy, the act of knitting, stitching, crochet, illustration and writing take me back to memories of being at home with my mother and my family, and all the feelings of warmth, comfort and security I associate with those early years. I am from a large family, and my mother was at its heart. Apart from domestic jobs, she would knit, sew and crochet, as well as using accessible and found objects from the domestic environment to create new from old — recycling was already well underway long before it became the societal norm it is now.

In hand-making the objects and creatures, I can always guarantee a different feeling or mood will get translated through the mistakes and imperfections inherent in the work, depending upon my current state of being at the time of creating the piece.

The toys and creatures become art through their individuality and their capacity to provoke a shared experience in the audience; people are invited to feel something through the project that they cannot buy in a shop.

Wishing you good knitting.
ARTURO AZCONA

YARNZAC

NATION

CUPCAKES

· ·

At the supermarket, a **CUPCAKE** caught my eye –
not because she was wearing stripy socks and
shiny shoes, but because she was looking very
sad. As I got closer, I saw that she wasn't the
only Cupcake, and that
all the others looked
equally miserable.

Even though each cupcake owned many pairs of beautiful shoes, they still felt unhappy. Shoes weren't making the Cupcakes happy due to a much bigger problem: they were quite empty inside because the baker had not put any filling inside them!

The solution? I knitted them some perfect pastry cream hearts.

TURN TO PAGE 96
FOR PATTERN

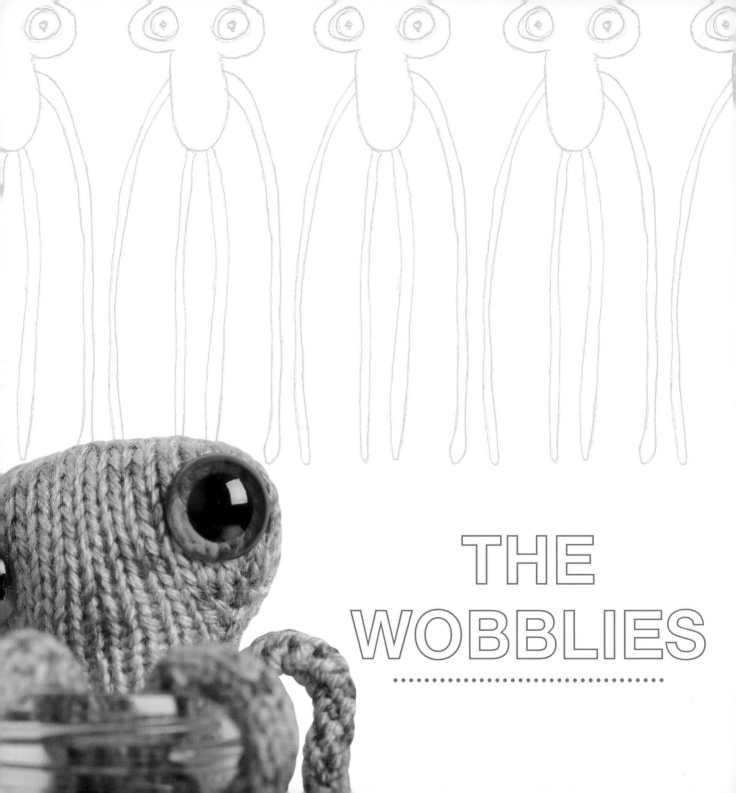

THE WOBBLIES

I found the **WOBBLY** at the park. He was lonely and upset and longed to be able to run, jump and play.

But his wobbly arms and legs made this impossible. I decided my next experiment would be to make his arms and legs strong so the Wobbly would not be wobbly any more.

THE RESULT

The original Wobbly wanted stronger limbs. Unfortunately, I was unable to help. So I cloned the Wobbly several times, although the cloning procedure did not produce stronger arms and legs.

However, the Wobbly now has others just like him who he can play with, and he is happy with that!

TURN TO PAGE 98 FOR PATTERN

SNOWFLAKE

One day I went to Nana's attic,

where I found a dusty top hat (Nana had

once worked as a magician's assistant).

As I picked up the hat to try it on, I noticed it

was quite heavy. I looked closer and snuggled

at the bottom of the hat was a white rabbit.

She told me her name was SNOWFLAKE.

Snowflake said she was too scared to leave the hat now that the magician had gone. I took Snowflake and the hat to my laboratory. After several days of observation and psychoanalysis, I discovered Snowflake had developed a severe case of agoraphobia.

Supercarrotsfragiletasticexpialipower

THE SOLUTION

It was clear to me that she needed confidence and strength to be able to leave the hat. I made knitted carrots using a special formula I had first developed as a medical student.

SUPERCA
RROT FR
AGILISTI
CEXPIAL
I POWER

After eating several of the special carrots, Snowflake felt able to leave the hat for the first time in years!

TURN TO
PAGE 100 FOR
PATTERN

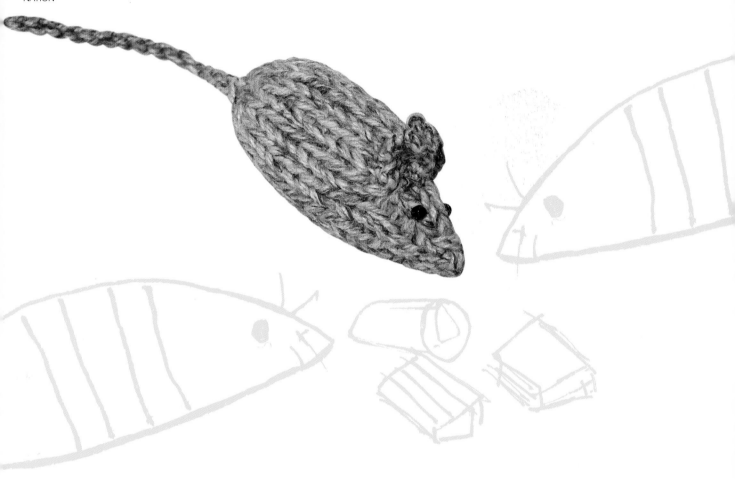

ALLSORTS MICE

I have a sweet indulgence: LIQUORICE ALLSORTS.

There's always a good supply in my laboratory. I

had put a family of bored and unhappy MICE in

an observation jar until I could come up with some

ideas of how to help them. I was thinking and

thinking, but all that came to mind was liquorice.

So I opened the drawer where I keep my allsorts.

The bag of liquorice caught, ripped open and

spilled out everywhere.

Thank you, Dr Knit! Thank you, Dr Knit!

AN UNEXPECTED RESULT

I grabbed a jar and quickly collected all the liquorice inside it, but I didn't realise that I'd taken the jar that contained the Mice. The morning after, I went to inspect the Mice, when suddenly, very colourful Mice jumped out of the jar squeaking: "Thank you, Dr Knit! Thank you, Dr Knit!" At the laboratory, something that went wrong turned out to be quite all right.

TURN TO
PAGE 102 FOR
PATTERN

THE RING BROTHERS

I first met the **RING BROTHERS** in a shop selling woollen jewellery. They were asking the shopkeeper if he knew how they could disentangle. I couldn't help overhearing, and I invited them to visit my laboratory where I introduced them to some other creatures.

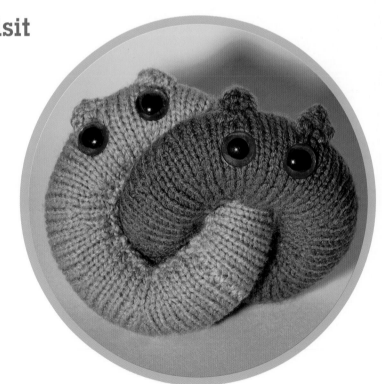

They were very excited to hear about my successful separation of Siamese bunnies, although I had to explain to them that a disentangling procedure was potentially more complicated. But, knowing that the Ring Brothers could have a happier life apart, we decided to go ahead with the procedure.

THE RESULT

The disentanglement was not at all easy, but it was not beyond my capability. After a couple of hours of complicated stitching and knitting work, the operation was a complete success. The Ring Brothers were very happy as they realised they now had the option to be together or apart, but no longer entangled!

TURN TO PAGE
103 FOR
PATTERN

ALL AT SEA
....
NO MORE
....

DEAN AND MARTIN

DEAN and MARTIN know that there's more

to life than sea life. They wanted to leave the

ocean and see big cities with high buildings.

But they couldn't breathe out of water.

AIR MARKER

OXYGEN CANISTER

O_2 FORMULA

I helped them by inventing a machine to teach them how to breathe oxygen.

Dean and Martin loved to spend hours in my machine, and, with practice, they learned how to breathe.

Then, we faced a second problem: Dean and Martin couldn't walk on land. However, I realised that because they're both pocket-sized, all I needed to do was to find some worthy humans to carry them around...I am sure that I'll be able to locate the right people for the job.

TURN TO
PAGE 104 FOR
PATTERN

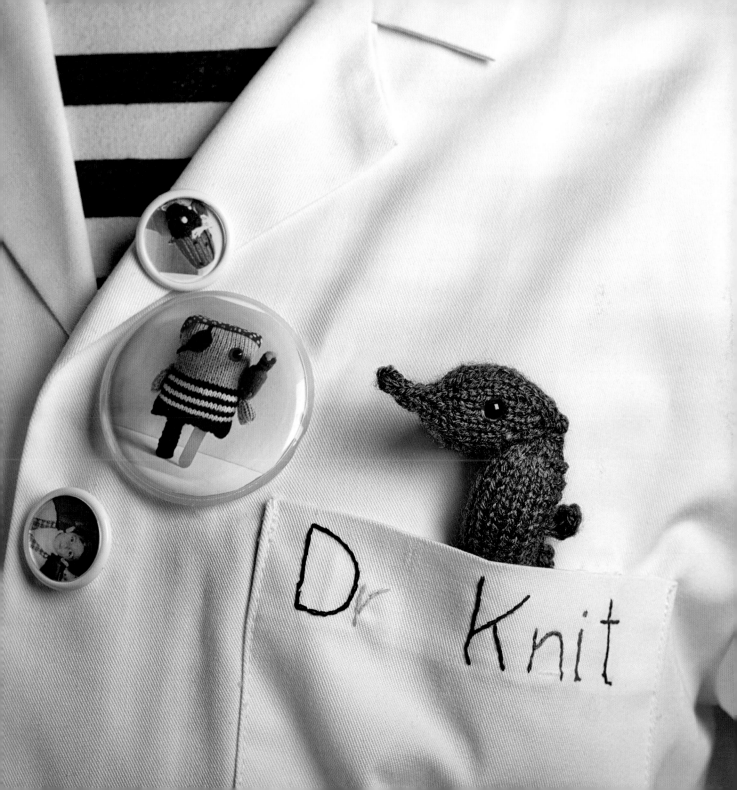

PIRATE THING

I was walking by the riverbank when I heard something crying. Nestled in some long grass was a strange, square-shaped thing. He wore a stripy top, an eye patch and had a wooden leg – just like a PIRATE! When I asked him why he seemed so lost, he couldn't remember.

I took him back to the laboratory, where I noticed that he seemed old and very tired. Something was missing, but it was difficult to tell quite what. After he had calmed down, he confided that he believed that he had nothing more to look forward to. When he was young, he'd sailed the seven seas and had many exciting adventures. Just talking about what was now past and gone, Pirate Thing became even more nostalgic and sad.

To help him, I gathered together bits and pieces from around the laboratory, including newspaper, cardboard and, of course, just the right kind of yarn. I created what I hoped would give Pirate Thing back the excitement he had lost. When I presented him with a new ship and a parrot companion, he was very happy. I told him how important it was for us to hold onto our sense of adventure.

A younger-looking Pirate Thing jumped into his ship, gave me a big smile and waved goodbye.

TURN TO
PAGE 106 FOR
PATTERN

THE ECO NARWHAL

· ·

Norman, a NARWHAL from the North, spotted a problem in his community: a lot of plastic rubbish was appearing in the oceans, and narwhals were getting it stuck on their tusks, causing them a lot of pain.

One day, despite his efforts to avoid the plastic, it happened to Norman. Clever as he was, he thought: "This is a case for calling Dr Knit."

So I travelled North, and brought Norman and a friend back to my laboratory.

Releasing the Narwhals from the plastic was easy (and of course I disposed of it safely, in the recycling bin), but they couldn't run the risk of this happening again. They needed to develop more confidence and skill in using their tusks to navigate and escape from the rubbish. I decided that knitting could be a wonderful exercise for them, and taught Norman and his friend how to knit with their tusks.

Once Norman and his friend had learned the art of knitting, the two of them could then teach the other Narwhals back home.

Norman had an even better solution, which was to stop the rubbish getting into the oceans in the first place, and I promised to spread his message to the world: "Please re-use, recycle and throw away less rubbish."

TURN TO PAGE
108 FOR
PATTERN

"Please re-use, recycle and throw away less rubbish."

TAKING
FLIGHT

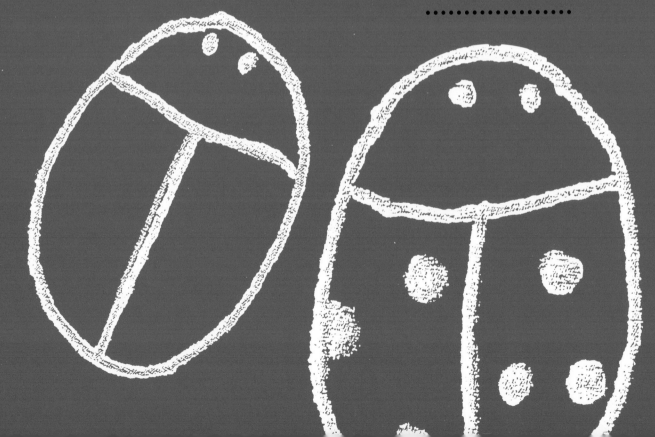

DOTTY
· · · · · · · · · · · · · · · · · ·

DOTTY is a very special ladybird and a little bit different: she has no dots! This made her Ma and Pa very concerned. They'd heard about my laboratory and got in touch in the hope that I could help.

I placed Dotty under observation while her worried Ma and Pa looked on. After several therapy sessions, I came to the conclusion that, yes, Dotty is different, and, yes, Dotty has no dots, but this isn't really a problem.

DOTTY is happy to be different.

She's a confident little ladybird just as she is. Ma and Pa were no longer worried about Dotty, but only after they themselves had received a free therapy session from Dr Knit!

TURN TO
PAGE 110 FOR
PATTERN

HIBOU THE OWL

HIBOU THE OWL came to me with impaired vision. Everything he saw was so beautiful that sometimes he felt dizzy. And sometimes he couldn't see anything at all.

THE SOLUTION

To rest Hibou's eyes, I tried a blindfold, but nothing changed. Next, I suggested prescription spectacles, but this produced only a slight improvement, although mainly because he now looked very sweet. Then, after administering psychoanalysis, I discovered the problem. He was not blind. He was blind to love!

Now that Hibou the Owl understands that this is the problem, his vision has cleared completely.

He is happy, in love, and sees the world through different eyes.

TURN TO
PAGE 112 FOR
PATTERN

LEONARDO DA KIWI

LEONARDO is a little Kiwi from New Zealand. He is a dreamer, and very clever. Leonardo is a bird with a difference. Like all Kiwis, he has no wings, but he has always dreamed that one day he will be able to fly.

One day he was in Wellington Town Library looking through a book titled *Great Men of Art and Science*. It was here that he came across two names: Leonardo da Vinci and Dr Knit.

Looking through Leonardo da Vinci's drawings and inventions he saw a pair of wings. He also saw that I had helped a lot of creatures overcome their problems. Putting two and two together he contacted me.

I was so happy when I received Leonardo's letter, as I like a challenge. I decided to help and invited Leonardo to my knitting laboratory.

THE RESULT

At the laboratory, myself and Leonardo studied the drawings and plans of Leonardo da Vinci's wings. After hours of study, I was able to develop super-light and super-strong knitted wings.

After solving a few technical problems, the wings worked and Leonardo was able to fly back to New Zealand.

Before he flew off, Leonardo promised to return to visit me again one day.

TURN TO
PAGE 114 FOR
PATTERN

NOT SO
CREEPY
CRAWLIES

SNAKES AND THE CITY

One morning, as I was having breakfast and reading my newspaper, I noticed an alarming story about a rapid increase in missing toys. I decided to investigate the mystery, and discovered that a large number of countryside SNAKES had found their way into city homes.

When the city children were at school, the Snakes would take the opportunity to play with their toys. They would play and play and play, and sometimes they would get so carried away that they would swallow the toys whole. This explained the disappearance of the toys, but also why the Snakes had such terrible indigestion!

I invited the Snakes to my laboratory for further observation. I was then able to propose a solution to extract the toys without hurting the Snakes and successfully treat their tummy ache.

After several therapy sessions, the Snakes learned how to control their impulse to swallow toys. This made the city children very happy indeed.

TURN TO
PAGE 116 FOR
PATTERN

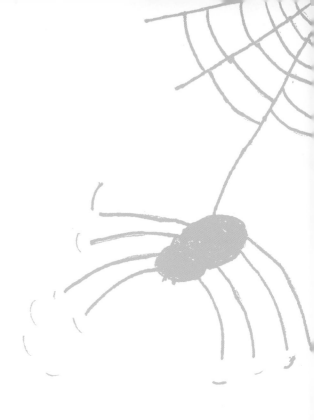

TINA TREMBLE

· ·

TINA TREMBLE, the trembling spider, was passing through the knitting laboratory when she heard some other creatures making plans for a Halloween party. She thought it would be funny to drop in and give them all a fright, but ever since she could remember she had always appeared frightened because she trembled so much.

After hearing about her difficulty, I decided to help. I put her under observation and discovered the reason why Tina Tremble trembled. It was bad circulation. She didn't tremble because she was scared...

...she trembled because she was cold!

THE SOLUTION

I decided to design special-sized, super-comfy legwarmers, a stylish pointy hat and a long wraparound scarf for her. Now Tina doesn't tremble any more, and she loves her new party outfit.

TURN TO
PAGE 118 FOR
PATTERN

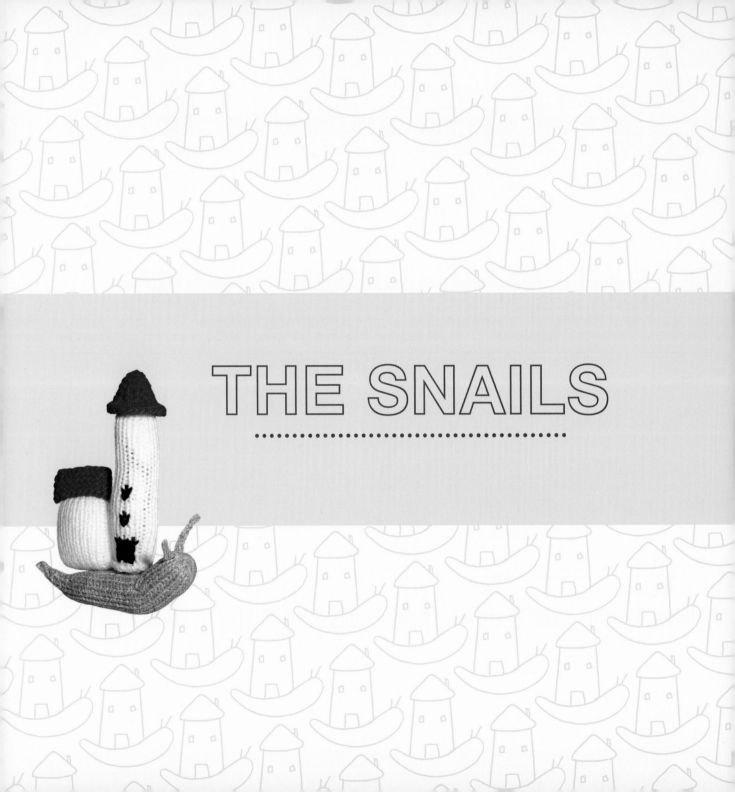

THE SNAILS

· ·

I was trekking deep in a dark and humid forest when I saw a procession of little moving houses. On closer inspection, I realised that they were SNAILS. They were very friendly, and I started chatting with them. Almost all of them told me how tired and exhausted they were from carrying their houses day after day.

THE SOLUTION

I told the Snails I might be able to help, and invited three of them back to my laboratory, where I observed them for five days. Finally, an idea came to me. I would create a cul-de-sac for the houses to be parked in, allowing the Snails to roam freely during the day.

The Snails were worried about feeling too exposed without anything on their backs, so I developed specially formulated lightweight pompoms as daytime replacements.

The Snails loved the idea of pompoms on condition they could choose their own colours.

TURN TO
PAGE 120 FOR
PATTERN

HONEY BEE MINE

Bees are very good to us. They pollinate the flowers and trees. They create wax for candles and lovely sweet honey. And sometimes they give us messages. One day, I was sitting in my laboratory, when I heard a noise. I turned around and at a table nearby I found a jar with three objects inside: a heart, a bee and a honey dipping stick.

DR KNIT CRACKS THE CODE

A honey dipping stick, a heart and a bee...a bee, a heart and a honey dipping stick...a honey dipping stick, a heart and a bee... honey...a bee...and a heart...HONEY BEE MINE!

I was very surprised and happy with the message, and suddenly realised what day it was...Valentine's Day, 14th of February. I wonder who sent this message to Dr Knit? Everybody needs a honey.

TURN TO
PAGE 122 FOR
PATTERN

Are bees messengers of love? I like to think so. They are also perfect examples of beings who live happily in communities and work in harmony.

THE KNITTING
LABORATORY

Basic techniques

There are no measurements of the creatures or examples of tension (gauge) for you to worry about. Creatures come in all shapes and sizes, so you can't go wrong. The same is true of the colour of yarn. These creatures are made with whatever you have handy and any colour you like.

SAFETY

Detached, small parts, such as this pirates's leg or eye, could choke a child or otherwise pose a safety risk. Do not give these creatures to children under the age of three. Even if you are giving these to kids over the age of three, make sure that you use safety eyes rather than beads or stuck-on eyes to avoid the need for medical intervention.

Casting on

There are many ways to cast on. Here are two methods, both of which start with the slipknot.

MAKING A SLIPKNOT

1 The slipknot is the first stitch of your knitting. Make a loop by passing the right side of the yarn over the left.

2 Take the tail end and make a second loop through the centre of the first loop.

3 Pull the tail end to secure the slipknot.

CASTING ON WITH TWO NEEDLES

Now put your left needle (or right if you are left-handed) through the slipknot and pull it tight. Now you are ready to cast on.

1 Put the right needle into the loop so that it passes under the left-hand needle. You are forming a cross with your needles, and the right-hand needle is at the back.

2 Wrap the yarn around the back needle coming between the needles. Take the yarn through the first loop with the back needle. This is your new stitch.

3 Put this new stitch on the left needle, next to the previous stitch.

4 Now you have two stitches. Repeat by putting the right-hand needle into the last stitch on the left-hand needle, and keep making stitches until you have enough.

CASTING ON THUMB METHOD

This is casting on using one needle and your thumb, sometimes called the 'long tail' method. You'll see why.

1 Use the short end of the yarn, and make it at least three times as long as your required cast-on edge.

2 Make a slipknot and place the loop on your left thumb.

3 Take the long length of yarn in your right hand and wrap the yarn around the point of the needle and between your thumb and the needle.

4 Draw the thread through the loop on the thumb, and then slip the loop over the edge of the needle. You have now knitted the slipknot, and are ready to make another stitch.

5 Repeat until you have the right amount of stitches.

Binding off

Binding off, or casting off, as it is also known in the UK, is a method to finish your knitting. If you don't finish it off properly it will all unravel, and you don't want that to happen. Always cast off in the appropriate way for your work, like knitted on a knit row, or purl on a purl row. If you are casting off in rib, follow the same pattern.

1 When you are ready to cast off, knit the first two stitches of the row. With the left needle, lift the first stitch over the top of the second stitch and let it go.

2 You now are down to one stitch on your right needle. Knit one more stitch and repeat step 1. When the last stitch remains, cut the yarn and pass the tail through the last stitch.

3 Where you are making a creature you can use the threading method to finish. When you get the the end of the knitting, break the yarn leaving a longish end. Thread this through all the remaining stitches using a tapestry needle. Pull this firmly and use the end to start sewing up the creature.

Basic stitches

The knit stitch and purl stitch are the basis of all knitting. Once you have mastered these, you are free to knit almost any pattern. Knitting or purling every row makes garter stitch. If you alternate knit and purl rows, you form stocking stitch (stockinette stitch), the most common of all stitches.

KNIT STITCH

Cast on the right amount of stitches for your project. With knitting, the yarn is always held at the back and your right-hand needle goes through the loop from front to back.

1 Insert the point of the right needle, from front to back, through the first loop on the left needle. You are forming a cross with your needles.
2 Draw the new loop through to the front of the work. Do this by pulling the left needle under the right one, pulling the new loop with it.
3 You have now made a new stitch, which is on the right-hand needle, and you need to drop the old one down to the row below. Keeping the tension with your finger, slip the old stitch off the left needle.
4 With your new stitch on the right-hand needle, repeat this whole process again until the end of the row. Turn your needles around so that all the stitches are held in your left hand again. The right needle is empty and ready to take on a whole new row.

PURL STITCH

Purl is done on the wrong side of the work when you are doing stocking stitch. Obviously, it is the right side of the work if you are doing reverse stocking stitch. If you work every row in purl it is garter stitch, just as if you had done all knit rows.

1 Bring your yarn to the front of your work. Insert the point of the right needle from back to front, through the first loop on the left needle.
2 Pass the yarn, which is held at the front of your work, between the two points of the needles.
3 Draw the loop through to the back of the work.
4 Slip the old stitch off the left-hand needle and repeat to the end of the row.

INCREASES

The increases are made by picking up a stitch from the row below. You can do that or make a stitch by working into the front and the back of the same stitch. The patterns do this mostly on the purl rows, but you can do it on the other side if you like. As long as you knit one row and purl the next you will still have the same result.

DECREASES

This is where you reduce the number of stitches by knitting or purling two or more stitches together. This will make the shape that you are knitting smaller. If you can, it's best to work all your decreases and increases in a similar place, like at the edge of a row, so it makes a satisfying pattern when you are finished.

Fastening off

1 After finishing the last stitch, snip off the yarn from the ball, leaving a couple of inches to weave in.

2 Using your needle or crochet hook, draw through the tail, pulling tightly to fasten.

Embroidery

Embroidery is an effective way of giving your creatures some added character and expression. It may help to use a blunt knitter's needle as this will not split the yarn as embroidery needles do, and will slip through the stitches easily.

Plastic eyes

These are available in all sorts of sizes. When your creature is near completion, glue them on with PVA (white glue). You can also buy safety eyes that are like a stud you push through the fabric and fix on the other side with a stopper.

Making up

Use a blunt-tipped tapestry needle or a needle designed for sewing knitted fabrics and yarn from your toy. You can use backstitch, oversewing or mattress stitch to join the pieces. Stuff the toy as you go. Insert your needle under the first stitch on the bound-off edge, bring the yarn over and insert it into the first stitch on the opposite bound-off edge. For a neat finish work into the first row only each time and keep each stitch the same length.

Abbreviations

Knitting

P – purl

K – knit

rem – remaining

sts – stitches

P2tog – purl 2 together

K2tog – knit 2 together

M1 – make 1 (pick up and knit (or purl) stitch
between needles)

CO – cast on

BO – bind or cast off

St st – stocking (stockinette) stitch

Cont – continue

alt – alternate

kfb – inc by knitting into the front and back of the st

Yoh – yarn over hook

dc – double crochet

sc – single crochet

ss – slip stitch

Crochet

US	UK	
sl st	sl st	slip stitch
ch	ch	chain
sc	dc	single crochet = UK double crochet
dc	tr	double crochet = UK treble
tr	dtr	treble = UK double treble

Yarns

USA	UK
Fingering	4 ply
Sport	Double knit
Bulky	Chunky

Knitting needles

US	METRIC (MM)	OLD UK
0	2	4
1	2.25	13
--	2.5	--
2	2.75	12
--	3	11
3	3.25	10
4	3.5	--
5	3.75	9
6	4	8
7	4.5	7
8	5	6
9	5.5	5
10	6	4
10.5	6.5	3
--	7	2
--	7.5	1
11	8	0
13	9	00
15	10	000

Crochet hooks

US	METRIC
B-1	2
C-2	2.75
D-3	3.25
E-4	3.5
F-5	3.75
G-6	4
7	4.5
H-8	5
J-9	5.5
J-10	6
K-10.5	6.5
L-11	8
M/N-13	9
N/P-15	10

Basic Crochet Techniques

HOW TO GET STARTED

The basics of crochet are very simple. Once you have made a basic chain, you are well on your way as even the most complicated and decorative stitches are just variations on this simple stitch. The following instructions are all for a right-handed person.

MAKE A SLIPKNOT

1 Make a loop in the yarn. With your crochet hook catch the ball end of the yarn and draw through loop.
2 Pull firmly on the yarn and hook to tighten the knot and create the first loop.

MAKING A CHAIN

1 To make a chain, hold the tail end of the yarn with the left hand and bring the yarn over the hook (yoh) by passing the hook in front of the yarn, under and around it.
2 Keeping the tension in the yarn taut, draw the hook and yarn through the loop.
3 Pull the yarn and hook through the hole and begin again, ensuring that the stitches are fairly loose. Repeat to make the number of chain required. As the chain lengthens, keep hold of the bottom edge to maintain the tension.

HOW TO COUNT A CHAIN

To count the stitches, use the right side of the chain, or the side that has more visible and less twisted 'v' shapes. Don't count the original slip stitch, but count each 'v' as one chain.

MAKE A SLIP STITCH (SS)

A slip stitch is used to join one stitch to another or a stitch to another point, as in joining a circle, and is usually made by picking up two strands of a stitch. However, where it is worked into the starting chain only pick up the back loop.

1 Insert the hook into the back loop of the next stitch and pass the yarn over the hook (yoh), as in chain stitch.
2 Draw the yarn through both loops on the stitch and repeat.

DOUBLE CROCHET (DC; SINGLE CROCHET – SC)

The hook is passed through the whole stitch (two strands).

1 Insert the hook front to back into the next stitch, two strands and one loop on the hook. Yoh.
2 Draw through to the front, two loops on the hook.
3 Yoh.
4 Draw through both loops to complete a single crochet. Work one sc into every stitch to the end.

WORKING IN THE ROUND: MAKING A CHAIN RING

There are two ways to begin circular crochet – with a chain or a loop. Work a chain as long as required by the pattern. Join the last chain to the first with a slip stitch. Begin the first round by working into each chain stitch.

WORKING IN THE ROUND: MAKING A YARN LOOP, OR MAGIC RING

This way of working in the round ensures that there is no hole in the middle of the work, as there is with a chain ring.

1 Make a loop with the tail end of the yarn on the right, the ball end on the left.

2 Pull the ball end through the loop (you will need to steady the work with your hand).

3 Make one chain through the loop on the hook you have drawn through to steady the round.

4 Work as many dc (sc) or whatever stitch you are using into the loop as is required by the pattern.

5 Pull the ends of the yarn tight to draw in the circle so that you have no hole in the middle of the first round.

Cupcake

MATERIALS

- 3.25 mm (US 3) needles
- Sponge-coloured DK (sport) yarn (beige)
- Icing-coloured DK (sport) yarn (white)
- Cherry-coloured DK (sport) yarn (red)
- Pink DK (sport) yarn (for nose and socks)
- Plastic doll's arms
- 1 pair of 14 mm safety eyes
- Tapestry or yarn needle
- Scissors
- Toy stuffing (Polyfill)

The procedure

BODY

Using beige yarn, CO 8 sts.

Row 1 and every alt row: K.

Row 2: M1, p8, m1 (10 sts).

Row 4: P2, (m1, p1) 6 times, p2 (16 sts).

Row 6: P3, (m1, p1) 10 times, p3 (26 sts).

Row 8: (P3, m1, p1) 6 times, p2 (32 sts).

Row 10: (P3, m1, p1) 8 times (40 sts).

Row 12: (P5, m1, p1) 6 times, p4 (46 sts).

Row 14: (P6, m1, p1) 6 times, p2 (50 sts).

Row 16: (P7, m1, p1) 6 times, p2 (56 sts).

Row 18: (P8, m1, p1) 6 times, p2 (62 sts).

Row 19-21: K.

Continue straight in St st for 18 rows.

Change to white yarn and begin decreases.

Row 40: (P8, p2tog) 6 times, p2 (56 sts).

Row 41 and every alt row: K.

Row 42: (P5, p2tog) 8 times (48 sts).

Row 44: (P6, p2tog) 6 times (42 sts).

Row 46: (P5, p2tog) 6 times (36 sts).

Row 48: (P4, p2tog) 6 times (30 sts).

Row 50: (P1, p2tog) 8 times, p6 (22 sts).

Row 52: (P2tog) 8 times, p6 (14 sts).

Row 54: (P2tog) 7 times (7 sts).

Break yarn and thread through rem sts.

LEGS

Using white yarn, CO 4 sts.

Work 2 rows St st in white, then change to pink (or other colour) for 2 rows.

Change to white and continue, making 7 coloured stripes alternating with white stripes.

Change to beige yarn and continue for 32 cm (12 ins).

Change to white yarn and repeat stripe pattern.

Bind off.

CHERRY

Using red yarn, CO 4 sts.

Work 4 rows St st.

Break yarn and thread through remaining sts.

MAKING UP THE CUPCAKE

Attach the eyes following manufacturer's instructions. Sew up the back of the cupcake, stuffing as you go, and fix the cherry on the top. Using pink yarn and a tapestry needle, embroider a small nose, using the photograph as a guide. Fold the legs in the middle and sew to the base of your cupcake. Make a hole in the top of each arm. Using your tapestry needle, thread a strong length of yarn through one arm, through the centre of the cupcake and through the second arm. Tie off the yarn at either end so that the arms retain some movement.

PASTRY HEART (MAKE 2)

Using beige yarn, CO 2 sts.

Row 1: K1, m1, k1 (3 sts).

Row 2: P3.

Row 3: M1, k3, m1 (5 sts).

Row 4 and every alt row: P.

Row 5: M1, k5, m1 (7 sts).

Row 7: M1, k7, m1 (9 sts).

Row 9: M1, k9, m1 (11 sts).

Row 11: M1, k11, m1 (13 sts).

Row 13: M1, k13, m1 (15 sts).

Row 15: K2tog, k11, k2tog (13 sts).

Row 16: P13.

Row 17: K2tog, k5. Turn, leaving remaining 6 sts on a stitch holder.

Row 18: P6.

Row 19: K2tog, k2, k2tog (4 sts).

Row 20: P4.

Row 21: Bind off.

Rejoin yarn to remaining 6 sts and reverse shaping on the other side.

Next row: P6.

Next row: K2tog, k2, k2tog (4 sts).

Next row: P4.

Next row: Bind off.

Make another heart shape and sew both together, stuffing as you go.

The Wobblies

MATERIALS

- 3.25 mm (US 3) needles
- Space-dyed DK (sport) yarn
- 1 pair of 2 cm safety eyes
- Tapestry or yarn needle
- Scissors
- Toy stuffing (Polyfill)

The procedure

BODY (MAKE 1)

CO 8 sts.

Work 2 rows St st.

Row 3: M1, k8, m1 (10 sts).

Work 15 rows St st.

Rows 19-24: Inc 1 st at each end of every row 6 times (22 sts).

Work 4 rows St st.

Decrease 1 st at each end of every row 6 times (10 sts).

Work 2 rows St st.

Now reverse the shaping to match by increasing 1 st at each end of every row 6 times (22 sts).

Work 4 rows St st.

Decrease 1 st at each end of every row 6 times (10 sts).

Work 15 rows St st.

Decrease 1 st at each end of next row.

Work 2 rows St st.

Bind off.

LEGS (MAKE 2)

CO 5 sts.

Row 1: K.

Row 2: K1, p3, k1.

Continue in this pattern for 130 rows. Bind off.

ARMS (MAKE 2)

CO 4 sts.

Row 1: K.

Row 2: K1, p2, k1.

Continue in this pattern for 150 rows. Bind off.

MAKING UP

Attach the eyes to the head, following the manufacturer's instructions. Fold the body in half and sew up the sides, adding the stuffing as you go. Attach the arms to both sides of the body and the legs to the thinnest part of the base. Wibbly, wobbly.

Snowflake

MATERIALS

- 5 mm (US 8) needles
- Bouclé yarn in white
- Oddments of pink and black DK (sport) yarn
- Orange and green DK (sport) yarn for carrot
- 1 pair of 12 mm safety eyes
- Tapestry or yarn needle
- Scissors
- Toy stuffing (Polyfill)

The procedure

BODY (MAKE 1)

Using white yarn, CO 6 sts.

Work in St st and increase 1 st on 4th and following alt rows until you have 10 sts.

M1 at each end of next row (12 sts).

Cont straight in St st until completed 69 rows altogether.

Decrease 1 st at either end of next row (10 sts).

Continue in St st and decrease 1 st on every alt row until you have 6 sts.

Work 2 rows and bind off.

HEAD (MAKE 1)

CO 8 sts and K 1 row.

Row 2: (P1, m1, p1) 4 times (12 sts).

Row 3 and every alt row: St st.

Row 4: (P2, m1, p1) 4 times (16 sts).

Row 6: (P1, m1, p1) 6 times, p4 (22 sts).

Row 8: (P2, m1, p1) 6 times, p4 (28 sts).

Row 10: (P6, m1, p1) 4 times (32 sts).

Row 12: (P7, m1, p1) 4 times (36 sts).

Row 14: M1, p36, m1 (38 sts).

Rows 15-17: St st.

Row 18: (P7, p2tog) 4 times, p2 (34 sts).

Row 20: (P6, p2tog) 4times, p2 (30 sts).

Row 22: (P5, p2tog) 4 times, p2 (26 sts).

Row 24: (P2, p2tog) 6 times, p2 (20 sts).

Row 26: (P3, p2tog) 4 times (16 sts).

Row 28: (P2tog) 6 times, p4 (10 sts).

Row 30: (P2tog) 5 times.

Break yarn and thread through remaining sts.

LEG (MAKE 2)

CO 9 sts.

Work in St st for 41 rows. On the next row and alt row m1 in each row (11 sts). Continue in St st and increase 1 st at either end of next and following alt rows 3 times (17 sts).

Rows 49–51: Work in st st straight.

Row 52: Inc 1 st at either end and 1 in middle of row (20 sts).

Row 53 and alt rows: P.

Row 54: Inc 2 st at either end of row (24 sts).

Row 56: Dec 1 st at either end of row (22 sts).

Row 58: Dec 1 st at either end of row (20 sts).

Row 60: Dec 2 st at either end of row (16 sts).

Row 61: (P2tog) 8 times (8 sts).

Break yarn and thread through remaining sts.

ARM (MAKE 2)

CO 8 sts.

Work in St st for 21 rows, increasing 1 st on 9th row (9 sts).

Row 22: Inc 1 st at either end of row (11 sts).

Row 23 and every alt row: St st.

Row 24: Inc 1 st at either end of row and inc 1 in middle of the row (14 sts).

Row 26: Inc 1 st at either end of row (16 sts).

Row 28: Dec 1 st at either end of row (14 sts).

Row 30: Dec 1 st at either end of row (12 sts).

Row 32: (P2tog) 6 times (6 sts).

Break yarn and thread through remaining sts.

EAR (MAKE 2)

CO 8 sts.

Work in St st for 20 rows, increasing 1 st on rows 12, 16 and 20 (11 sts).

Row 22: Inc 1 st at either end of row (13 sts).

Row 23 and every alt row: St st.

Row 24: Inc 1 st at either end of row and inc 1 in middle of the row (16 sts).

Row 26: Inc 1 st at either end of row (18 sts).

Row 28: Dec 1 st at either end of row (16 sts).

Row 30: Dec 2st at either end of row (12 sts).

Row 32: (P2tog) 6 times (6 sts).

Break yarn and thread through remaining sts.

MAKING UP

Sew up the head, body, arms and legs, stuffing as you go. Attach the eyes to the front of the head before you sew it up, then sew the body parts together, adding the ears to either side of the head. Sew eyelashes above the eyes in black, and a cross for a nose in pink yarn.

CARROT

Using 2 strands of orange yarn and 5 mm (US 8) needles, CO 4 st and work in St st for 4 rows.

Increase 1 st in next and following alt row (6 sts).

Continue in St st for another 5 rows.

Next row: M1, p6, m1 (8 sts).

Repeat this shaping 2 more times (12 sts).

Row 24: (P3, m1, p1) 3 times (15 sts).

Row 26: M1, p15 (16 sts).

Row 28: M1, p16, m1 (18 sts).

Work St st for 3 rows.

Row 32: (P2, p2tog) 4 times, p2 (14 sts).

Row 34: (P2tog) 7 times (7 sts).

Break yarn and thread through remaining sts.

Sew up the side of the carrot, adding stuffing as you go. To make the green top, make a crochet chain and fold into the centre or add tufts of green yarn to the top.

Allsorts Mice

MATERIALS

- 5 mm (US 8) needles
- Oddments of brown DK yarn
- Oddments of pink, black and yellow DK yarn
- Beads for eyes
- Tapestry or yarn needle
- Scissors, sewing needle and black thread
- Toy stuffing (Polyfill)

The procedure

BORING MOUSE BODY

Using 2 strands of brown yarn, CO 4.

Working in St st, increase 1 st at each end of every other row
4 times (12 sts).

Row 10: Inc 1 st at each end and 1 st in the middle of the row
(15 sts).

Continue in St st for another 13 rows.

Next row: (P2tog) 6 times, p3tog.

Break yarn and thread through remaining sts. Pull tight and
stitch seam.

EARS (MAKE 2)

Using 1 strand of brown yarn, CO 4 sts.

Work 6 rows in St st. Break yarn and pull sts tight. Attach to
either side of head.

TAIL

Take 2 strands of brown yarn 15 cm (10 in) long. Twist until
they fold in the centre.

ALLSORTS MOUSE

Make body as for Boring Mouse, but using bright coloured
yarns, until you have 15 sts. Working in St st, change colour
and work 4 rows in main colour, then a 4 row stripe and then
change back to main colour for rest of body, Alternatively,
alternate 2 rows in main colour and 2 in a contrast for 12 rows.

Next row: In the main body colour, (p2tog) 6 times, p3tog.
Break yarn and thread through remaining sts. Pull tight and
stitch seam.

MAKING UP

Stitch long edges of body together, stuffing as you go so that
seam is under body. Attach tail to fat end of body. Sew beads
for eyes on either side of head.

The Ring Brothers

MATERIALS

- 5 mm (US 8) needles
- 5 mm (US H-8) crochet hook
- Two colours of DK (sport) yarn
- 2 pairs of 2 cm safety eyes
- Tapestry or yarn needle
- Scissors
- Toy stuffing (Polyfill)

The procedure

BODY (MAKE 2)

Using 2 strands of yarn, CO 35 sts.

Row 1: P.

Row 2: K.

Row 3: P5, (m1, k12) 2 times, m1, k6 (38 sts).

Row 4: K9, m1, k20, m1, k9 (40 sts).

Row 5: P4, (m1, p8) 4 times, m1, p4 (45 sts).

Row 6: K11, m1, k23, m1, k11 (47 sts).

Row 7: P7, (m1, p16) 2 times, m1, p8 (50 sts).

Row 8 and every alt row: K.

Row 9: P8, (m1, p17) 2 times, m1, p8 (53 sts).

Row 11: P13, m1, p27, m1, p13 (55 sts).

Row 13: P14, m1, p27, m1, p14 (57 sts).

Row 15: P9, (m1, p19) 2 times, m1, p10 (60 sts).

Now reverse shaping.

Row 17: P9, (p2tog, p18) 2 times, p2tog, p9 (57 sts).

Row 19: P13, p2tog, p27, p2tog, p13 (55 sts).

Row 21: P13, p2tog, p26, p2tog, p12 (53 sts).

Row 23: P8, (p2tog, p16) 2 times, p2tog, p7 (50 sts).

Row 25: P7, (p2tog, p15) 2 times, p2tog, p7 (47 sts).

Row 26: K11, k2tog, k22, k2tog, k10 (45 sts).

Row 27: P4, (p2tog, p7) 4 times, p2tog, p3 (40 sts).

Row 28: K.

Row 29: P9, p2tog, p18, p2tog, p9 (38 sts).

Row 30: K5, (k2tog, k11) 2 times, k2tog, k5 (35 sts).

Purl 1 more row and bind off.

EARS (MAKE 4)

Using 2 strands of the same colour and crochet hook, make a magic ring and ch 16 into the centre. Fasten off. Make 3 more and fix to the widest point of your knitting.

MAKING UP

Fix the eyes beneath the ears, following the manufacturer's instructions. At this point you need to decide if your ring is solitary or if it is joined to its brother. Sew the short ends of your piece together, then stitch the inner circle. Leave a gap, stuff and then complete the stitching.

Dean and Martin

MATERIALS

- 3.25 mm (US 3) needles
- Blue DK (sport) yarn
- 2 pairs of 18 mm safety eyes
- Fine craft wire
- Pipe cleaner
- Tapestry or yarn needle
- Scissors
- Toy stuffing (Polyfill)

The procedure

BODY (MAKE 2)

Using blue yarn, CO 4 sts.

Work in garter st for 12 rows (k every row).

Row 13: Inc 1 st in this and following alt row (6 sts).

Continue in garter st for 10 rows.

Row 26: Inc 1 st in this row (7 sts).

Continue in garter st for 8 rows.

Row 35: Inc 1 st in this row (8 sts).

Continue in garter st for 7 rows.

Row 43: Inc at both ends of the row (10 sts).

Continue in garter st for 7 rows.

Row 51: Inc at both ends of the row (12 sts).

Row 52: K3, m1, p6, m1, k3 (14 sts).

Row 53: K2, m1, p10, m1, k2 (16 sts).

Row 54: K2, m2, p12, m2, k2 (20 sts).

Keeping pattern as set work another 19 rows straight.

Row 74: K4, (p2tog) 6 times, k4 (14 sts).

Row 75: K.

Row 76: K4, (p2tog) 3 times, k4 (11 sts).

Row 77: (P2tog) 5 times, k1 (6 sts).

Break off yarn and thread through remaining sts.

HEAD (MAKE 2)

Using blue yarn, CO 5 sts.

Rows 1-9: Working in St st inc 1 st on rows 6 and 8 (7 sts).

Rows 10-14: Inc 1 st at each edge on every row (17 sts).

Row 15-23: Cont in St st and inc 2 st at each edge on rows 14 and 16 (26 sts).

Continue in St st.

Row 24: Dec 2 sts at each edge (22 sts).

Row 26: Dec 2 sts at each edge (18 sts).

Row 28: Dec 2 sts at each edge (14 sts).

Row 30: (K2tog) 7 times (7 sts).

Break off yarn and thread through remaining sts.

FIN (MAKE 2)

CO 6 sts.

Rows 1-7: Knit every row and inc 1 st at each edge on rows 3, 5, and 7 (12 sts).

Row 8: K.

Row 9-13: K dec 1 st at each edge on rows 9 and 13 (6 sts).

Bind off.

MAKING UP

Attach the eyes to either side of the head, following the manufacturer's instructions. Sew the head pieces together, stuffing as you go. Insert the pipe cleaner into the body along the back to achieve the curling tail. Sew up the body, stuffing as you go. Sew the head to the body. Fold the fin in half and attach to the back of the seahorse, using the photograph as a guide to positioning.

. . . .

Pirate Thing

MATERIALS

- 5 mm (US 8) and 3.25 mm (US 3) needles
- Beige, black and white DK (sport) yarn
- Green, red, black and yellow yarn for the parrot
- Orange and black embroidery thread
- Small piece of black felt
- 2 cm safety eye
- Wooden tongue depressor or lolly stick
- Tapestry or yarn needle and embroidery needle
- Scissors
- Toy stuffing (Polyfill)

The procedure

PIRATE BODY (MAKE 1)

Using 2 strands of black yarn and 5 mm (US 8) needles, CO 40 sts.

Knit 6 rows in St st.

Row 7-8: Change to white and continue in St st.

Row 9-10: St st in black.

Row 11-12: St st in white.

Row 13-14: St st in black.

Row 15-16: St st in white.

Row 17-18: St st in black.

Change to beige and work 20 rows St st.

Bind off.

PIRATE LEG (MAKE 1)

Using 2 strands of black yarn and 5 mm (US 8) needles, CO 8 sts.

Work 30 rows in St st.

Bind off.

Fold in half lengthwise and sew up the side, stuffing as you go.

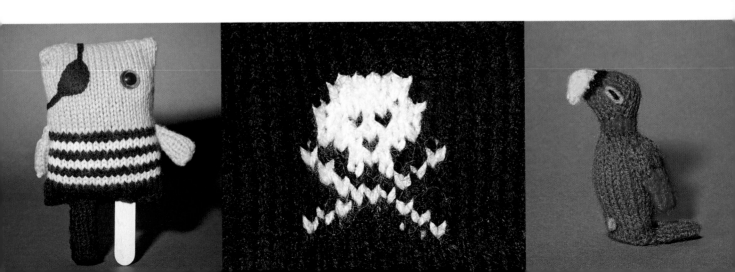

PIRATE ARMS (MAKE 2)

Using 2 strands beige yarn and 5 mm (US 8) needles, CO 7 sts.

Work 7 rows in St st.

Row 8: K2tog, k3, k2tog (5 sts).

Row 9: P.

Row 10: K2tog, k1, k2tog (3 sts).

Row 11: Bind off.

MAKING UP THE PIRATE

Fold the body rectangle and attach the eye to one side. Create a seam down the back, stuffing as you go. Attach the knitted leg to one side and insert the wooden leg on the other. Make a small hole in the wooden stick where it enters the body. Keeping half the stick inside the body, sew up the seam and pass the needle through the hole to secure it. Using the template on page 124, cut out the eye patch and attach. Fold each arm in half lengthwise. Stuff and attach to each side of the body.

JOLLY ROGER

Using a single strand of black yarn and 5 mm (US 8) needles, CO 30 sts.

Work 5 rows St st.

Following the chart on page 124, work the skull and cross-bones. Work another 5 rows of St st. Bind off.

PARROT BODY, HEAD AND TAIL (MAKE 1)

Using 1 strand green yarn and 3.25mm (US 3) needles, CO 5 sts.

Row 1: K1, p1, k1, p1, k1.

Row 2: P.

These 2 rows form the pattern for the tail. Repeat 4 times. At the same time increase 1 st at either end of the 4th row (7 sts).

Row 11: M3, p7 (10 sts).

Row 12: M3, k10 (13 sts).

Work in St st for 15 rows.

Row 16: M1, p13, m1 (15 sts).

Rows 17-19: St st.

Row 20: M1, p15, m1 (17 sts).

Rows 21-27: St st.

Row 28: P1, (p2tog, p2) 4 times (13 sts).

Row 29: K.

Row 30: P1, (p2tog, p1) 4 times (9 sts).

Changing to red yarn for neck, work 3 rows St st.

Change back to green for head.

Row 34: P3, (m1, p1) 3 times, p3 (12 sts).

Rows 35-37: St st.

Row 38: P8 sts and turn, leaving last 4 sts on the needle.

Row 39: K4, turn.

For next 2 rows work St st on the central 4 sts only.

Row 42: P8.

Row 43: K12.

Row 44-45: St st (12 sts).

Row 46: Change to red yarn, (p2tog) 2 times, p4, (p2tog) 2 times (8 sts).

Row 47: K.

Row 48-49: Using black yarn, work 2 rows St st.

Row 50: Change to yellow, p2tog at either end of the row (6 sts).

Rows 51-53: St st.

Row 54: P2tog at either end of row (4 sts).

Row 55: K.

Break the yarn and thread through the rem sts.

PARROT WINGS (MAKE 2)

Using 1 strand red yarn and 3.25 mm (US 3) needles, CO 3 sts. Work 7 rows St st, increasing 1 st on 3rd and 5th rows (5 sts). Change to green yarn and work a further 8 rows St st. Decrease 1 st in last row (4 sts). Bind off. Weave in loose ends.

MAKING UP THE PARROT

Embroider eyes where short-row shaping has left holes, using orange thread for surround and black for centre. Fold body in half lengthwise and sew along centre, stuffing as you go. Attach wings to either side of body.

The Eco Narwhal

MATERIALS

• 5.5 mm (US 9) and 3.25 mm (US 3) needles
• Flecked Aran (worsted) yarn
• Yellow DK yarn for the tusk
• Chopstick
• PVA (craft glue)
• 1 pair of 12 mm black safety eyes
• Tapestry or yarn needle
• Scissors
• Toy stuffing (Polyfill)

The procedure

BODY (MAKE 1)

Using flecked yarn and 5.5 mm (US 9) needles, CO 6 sts.

Row 1: K.
Row 2: (M1, p2) 3 times, m1 (10 sts).
Row 3: M1, k10, m1 (12 sts).
Row 4: (M1, p2) 6 times (18 sts).
Row 5: (M1, k6) 3 times, m1 (22 sts).
Row 6: P6, (m1, p1) 10 times, p2 (32 sts).
Row 7: K.
Row 8: M1, p5, (m1, p3) 7 times, m1, p4, m1, p2 (42sts).
Row 9: K.
Row 10: P30, (m1, p1) 10 times, p2 (52 sts).
Row 11: K.
Row 12: P48, (m1, p1) 4 times (56 sts).

Continue straight in St st for 19 rows.

Row 32: P2tog, p52, p2tog (54 sts).
Row 33 and every alt row: K.
Row 34: P2tog, p50, p2tog (52 sts).

Stay in St st and keep decreasing at the end of every other row until you have 38 sts. Then decrease at the end of every 4th row until you have 16 sts.

Break the yarn and thread through the remaining stitches.

TAIL (MAKE 1)

Using flecked yarn and 5.5 mm (US 9) needles, CO 22 sts.
Work 2 rows St st.
Decrease at both ends of every row until you have 8 sts.
Work 4 rows St st.
Increase at both ends of every row until you have 20 sts.
Work 1 row St st and bind off.

FLIPPERS (MAKE 2)

Using flecked yarn and 5.5 mm (US 9) needles, CO 2 sts.
Increase 1 st in every other row until you have 9 sts, then reverse shaping, decreasing every other row until you have 2 sts. Bind off. Fold in half and stuff, sewing the edges together.

TUSK

Using yellow yarn and 3.25 mm (US 3) needles, CO 5 sts. K for 16 cm (6 in) until you have enough to cover your chopstick.

Decrease 1 st every row until you have 2 st. Break the yarn and thread through the last 2 sts. Dip your chopstick in some PVA (craft glue) and roll it in the yellow tube, sewing along the length as you go.

MAKING UP

Attach the eyes and flippers. Stuff and sew up the long seam of the body. Insert the back end of the tusk inside the body so that 13 cm (5 in) protrudes and the rest is inside to hold the tusk firm. Fold the tail in half and stuff. Attach the short edge of the tail to the thin end of the body.

Dotty

MATERIALS

- 3.5 mm (US 4) needles
- Oddments of red and black DK (sport) yarn
- Sewing needle
- Scissors
- 3 pairs of 5 mm googly eyes
- Snippet of lace ribbon and matching thread
- Toy stuffing (Polyfill)

The procedure

MA AND PA

Using red yarn, CO 10 sts.

Row 1 and every alt row: K.

Row 2: M2, p10, m2 (14 sts).

Row 4: M1, k1, m1, p12, m1, k1, m1 (18 sts).

Row 6: K2, m1, p14, m1, k2 (20 sts).

Row 8: K3, p14, k3.

Continue straight in this pattern for a further 8 rows.

Change to black yarn.

Row 17 and alt rows: K.

Row 18: K3, p2tog, p10, p2tog, k3 (18 sts).

Row 20: K3, p2tog, p8, p2tog, k3 (16 sts).

Row 22: K2tog, k1, p2tog, p6, p2tog, k1, k2tog (12 sts).

Row 23: K2tog, k8, k2tog (10 sts).

Break yarn and thread through remaining sts.

MAKING UP MA AND PA

Use black yarn to stitch a line down the centre. This is the centre back. Embroider 3 dots either side. Attach eyes on the black head at the front. Use a snippet of lace or ribbon to create a ruff for mother ladybird. Sew a seam along the bottom of Ma and Pa and stuff as you go.

DOTTY SMALL

Using red yarn, CO 10 sts.

Row 1 and alt rows: K.

Row 2: K1, m1, p8, m1, k1 (12 sts).

Row 4: M2, k1, m1, p5, m1, p5, m2, k1 (18 sts).

Row 6: K3, p12, k3.

Continue straight in this pattern for another 8 rows.

Change to black yarn

Continue in pattern for 2 more rows.

Row 16: K2tog, K1, k2tog, p3, p2tog, p3, k2tog, k1, k2tog (13 sts).

Row 18: K2tog, p3, p2tog, p3, k1, k2tog (11 sts).

Row 19: K.

Break yarn and thread through remaining sts.

MAKING UP DOTTY SMALL

Use black yarn to make a line down the centre. This is the centre back. Attach the eyes on the black head at the front. Sew a seam along the bottom and stuff as you go.

Cactus

MATERIALS

- 5.5 mm (US 9) needles
- Green DK (sport) yarn
- Brown eyelash yarn
- Tapestry or yarn needle
- Scissors
- Toy stuffing (Polyfill)

CACTUS BODY 1

Using 1 strand of green and 1 of brown, CO 12 sts.

Row 1: K.

Row 2: (K1, p1) repeat to end.

These 2 rows form the pattern. Continue in pattern until your cactus is the right height.

Break yarn and thread through remaining sts.

CACTUS BODY 2

Make a second cactus. With 1 strand of green and 1 of brown, CO 10 sts.

Row 1: K.

Row 2: (K1, p1) repeat to end.

These 2 rows form the pattern. Continue in pattern until your cactus is the right height.

Break yarn and thread through remaining sts.

Cacti can be different sizes and as high as you like.

MAKING UP

The pattern will be different on each side of the fabric. Choose the one that you like best and sew up the sides of both cacti. Stuff and draw up the loose stitches at the base to finish.

Plant your cacti in a flower pot with some brown or green yarn for soil. Your ladybirds will enjoy sitting on it.

Hibou the Owl

MATERIALS

- 5 mm (US 8) needles
- White DK (sport) yarn
- Oddment of beige yarn
- Ready-made heart shapes or red felt
- 1 pair of 18 mm safety eyes
- Stitch holder or safety pin
- Tapestry or yarn needle
- Scissors
- Toy stuffing (Polyfill)

The procedure

BODY (MAKE 2)

Using 2 strands of white yarn, CO 20 sts.

Work in St st for 30 rows. Decrease 1 st at either end of rows 10 and 18 (16 sts).

Row 31: K4 and put these sts on a holder. BO 8 sts, k4.

Row 32: P1, p2tog, p1 (3 sts).

Row 33: K.

Row 34: P1, p2tog (2 sts).

Row 35: K.

Row 36: P2tog.

Bind off last st.

Put last 4 sts back on the needle and repeat shaping for the other ear:

Row 32: P1, p2tog, p1 (3 sts).

Row 33: K.

Row 34: P1, p2tog (2 sts).

Row 35: K.

Row 36: P2tog.

Bind off last st.

BASE (MAKE 1)

Using 2 strands of white, CO 13 sts.

Row 1 and alt rows: K.

Row 2: M1, p6, m1, p7, m1 (16 sts).

Row 4: M1, p8, m1, p8, m1 (19 sts).

Row 6: (P4, p2tog) 3 times, p1 (16 sts).

Row 8: (P3, p2tog) 3 times, p1 (13 sts).

Row 9: K.

Bind off.

WING 1 (MAKE 2)

Using 2 strands of white yarn, CO 5 sts.

Row 1: K.

Row 2: M1, p5, m1 (7 sts).

Row 3: M1, k7, m1 (9 sts).

Row 4: P8, kfb (inc by knitting into the front and back of the st) (10 sts).

Row 5: Kfb, k9 (11 sts).

Row 6: P10, kfb (12 sts).

Row 7: K11, kfb (13 sts).

Row 8: BO 3 sts, p8, p2tog (9 sts).

Row 9: K2tog, k5, k2tog (7 sts).

Bind off.

WING 2 (MAKE 2)

This is the same as Wing 1 with the shaping reversed. CO 5 sts.

Row 1: P.

Row 2: M1, k5, m1 (7 sts).

Row 3: M1, p7, m1 (9 sts).

Row 4: Kfb, k8 (10 sts).

Row 5: P9, kfb (11 sts).

Row 6: Kfb, k10 (12 sts).

Row 7: P11, kfb (13 sts).

Row 8: BO 3 sts, p8, p2tog (9 sts).

Row 9: K2tog, k5, k2tog (7 sts).

Bind off.

MAKING UP

Sew the wing halves together, stuffing as you go. Use the template on page 125 to cut out 2 hearts in red felt (or use ready-made fabric hearts). Position on the front of the head and attach safety eyes in the centre, following the manufacturer's instructions. Join the front and the back of the body together and sew around the edges, stuffing as you go. Embroider the beak and the feet in beige yarn.

Leonardo da Kiwi

MATERIALS

- 4.5 mm (US 7) and 3.25 mm (US 3) needles
- 4 mm (US G-6) crochet hook
- Brown and cream DK (sport) yarn
- Oddment of yellow yarn
- 1 pair of 9 mm safety eyes
- Pipe cleaner
- Card for wings
- Tapestry or yarn needle
- Scissors
- Toy stuffing (Polyfill)

The procedure

BODY (MAKE 1)

Using 2 strands brown yarn, 4.5 mm (US 7) needles, CO 8 sts.

Row 1 and every alt row: K.

Row 2: M1, p8, m1 (10 sts).

Row 4: M1, (p2, m1) 5 times (16 sts).

Row 6: P3, (p1, m1) 10 times, p3 (26 sts).

Row 8: P2, (m1, p4) 6 times (32 sts).

Row 10: (M1, p4) 8 times (40 sts).

Row 12: P5, (m1, p5) 6 times, p5 (46 sts).

Row 14: P21, (m1, p1) 4 times, p21 (50 sts).

Row 16: P22, (m1, p1) 6 times, p22 (56 sts).

Row 18: P26, (m1, p1) 4 times, p26 (60 sts).

Row 20: P29, (m1, p1) 2 times, p29 (62 sts).

Continue in St st for 11 rows.

Row 32: P2tog, p56, p2tog (60 sts).

Row 34: P7, (p2tog, p13) 3 times, p 2tog, p6 (56 sts).

Row 36: (P7, p2tog) 6 times, p2 (50 sts).

Row 38: (P6, p2tog) 6 times, p2 (44 sts).

Row 40: (P5, p2tog) 6 times, p2 (38 sts).

Row 42: (P2, p2tog) 8 times, p6 (30 sts).

Row 44: (P3, p2tog) 6 times (24 sts).

Row 46: (P2, p2tog) 6 times(18 sts).

Row 48: M1, p18, m1 (20 sts).

Row 50: P8, (m1, p1) 4 times, p8 (24 sts).

Row 52: P10, (m1, p1) 4 times, p10 (28 sts).

Row 54: M1, p28, m1 (30 sts).

Continue in St st for 7 rows.

Row 62: (P5, p2tog) 4 times, p2 (26 sts).

Row 64: (P2, p2tog) 6 times, p2 (20 sts).

Row 66: (P3, p2tog) 4 times (16 sts).

Row 68: P2, (P2tog) 6 times, p2 (10 sts).

Row 70: (P2tog) 5 times (5 sts).

Break yarn and thread through remaining sts.

Fix eyes to the head, following manufacturer's instructions.

Join seam and stuff as you go along.

BEAK AND LEGS (MAKE 3)

Using 2 strands of yellow yarn and 4.5 mm (US 7 needles),
CO 4 sts.

Work in St st for 21 rows.

Row 22: M1, p4 (5 sts).

Break yarn and tie off.

For the beak and legs insert pipe cleaners.

For the feet using 1 strand of yellow yarn and crochet hook ch 14.

Break yarn and fasten both ends to end of leg. Pull in middle to
make 2 toes and stitch to hold. Repeat for other leg.

WINGS (MAKE 4)

Using cream yarn and 3.25 mm (US 3) needles, CO 10 sts.

K 10 rows garter st.

Make all shaping on one edge.

Row 11: M1, k10 (11 sts).

Row 12: K.

Row 13: M1, k11 (12 sts).

Rows 14-18: K

Row 19: K2tog, K10 (11sts).

Row 20-22: K.

Row 23: M1, K11 (12 sts).

Row 24 and alt rows: K.

Increase 1 st at the same edge every alt row until you have 22 sts.

Begin decreases on the opposite edge by k2tog every row.

After 5 rows K2tog at both ends of the row.

After another 4 rows decrease at both ends of the row.

Continue to decrease until 1 st left, and bind off.

Repeat shape another 3 times. Using template on page 125,
cut out 2 wings in card. Stretch knitted shapes around card and
sew wing pieces along edges, enclosing card. Repeat for other
wing. Sew wings together at short edge; sew to back of body.

• • • • • • • • • • • • • •

Snakes and the City

MATERIALS

- 3.25 mm (US 3) needles
- Coloured DK (sport) yarn of your choice
- 12 mm safety eyes
- Red felt for tongue
- Tapestry or yarn needle
- Scissors
- Toys for stuffing: tennis ball, puzzle cube, toy car
- Toy stuffing (Polyfill)

The procedure

BODY OF TOY-FREE SNAKE

Using 1 strand of yarn, CO 6 sts.

To shape the head work in St st.

Row 1: K.

Row 2: M1, p6, m1 (8 sts).

Row 3: M1, k8, m1 (10 sts).

Row 4: M2, p10, m2 (14 sts).

Row 5: M1, k14, m1 (16 sts).

Row 6: M2, p16, m2 (20 sts).

Row 7: K.

Row 8: M2, p20, m2 (24 sts).

Row 9: M1, k24, m1 (26 sts).

Continue straight in St st for 8 rows.

Row 18: P2tog, p22, p2tog (24 sts).

Row 19: (K2tog) 2 times, k16, (k2tog) 2 times (20 sts).

Row 20: K2tog, p16, k2tog (18 sts).

Row 21: K2tog, p12, k2tog (16 sts).

For straight snake cont straight in St st until measures 50 cm (19½ in).

** Next row: (K2tog) 2 times, k6, (k2tog) 2 times (10 sts).

Work in St st for 3 rows.

Next row: K2tog, k6, k2tog (8 sts).

Work in St st for 3 rows.

Next row: K2tog, k4, k2tog (6 sts).

Work 1 row St st.

Next row: (K2tog) 3 times (3 sts).

Break off yarn and thread through remaining sts.

MAKING UP THE TOY-FREE SNAKE

Attach eyes, following manufacturer's instructions. Sew together body, stuffing as you go. Using template on page 124, cut out forked tongue in red felt and sew to head.

TENNIS BALL OR PUZZLE CUBE SNAKE

To make a snake that has swallowed a tennis ball or a puzzle cube, replace the central straight part of the snake pattern from Rows 22 until the work measures 50 cm (20 in) with the following shaping.

Row 1: K14.

Row 2: M1, (p2, m1) 7 times (22 sts).

Row 3: M1, k22, m1 (24 sts).

Row 4: (P6, m1) 4 times (28 sts).

Row 5: M1, k28, m1 (30 sts).

Row 6: (P7, m1) 4 times, p2 (34 sts).

Row 7: M1, k34, m1 (36 sts).

Row 8: M1, p36, m1 (38 sts).

Continue in St st inc 2 sts on every alt row 3 times (44 sts).

Row 16: (P12, m1) 4 times (52 sts).

Continue straight in St st for 5 rows then reverse shaping.

Row 22: (P9, p2tog) 4 times (48 sts).

Row 23: K.

Row 24: (P8, p2tog) 4 times (44 sts).

Row 25: K.

Row 26: P2, (p8, p2tog) 4 times, p2 (40 sts).

Row 27: K.

Row 28: (P6, p2tog) 4 times (36 sts).

Row 29: (K2tog) 2 times, k30, (k2tog) two times (32 sts).

Row 30: P2tog, p28, p2tog (30 sts)

Row 31: K.

Row 32: P2tog, p26, p2tog (28 sts).

Row 33: K.

Row 34: (P5, p2tog) 4 times (24 sts).

Row 35: K2tog, k20, k2tog (22 sts).

Row 36: P1, (p1, p2tog) 7 times (15 sts).

Work 2 rows St st. Continue with tail pattern, working from ** on page 116

Make up as for the toy-free snake (see opposite), but when you come to the central part of the snake's body, position a tennis ball or puzzle cube on the knitting and sew the body around it.

CAR SNAKE

To make a snake that has swallowed a car replace the central straight part of the snake pattern from Row 22 until the work measures 50 cm (19½ in) with the following shaping.

Row 1: K14.

Row 2: M1, (P2, m1) 7 times (22 sts).

Row 3: M1, k22, m1 (24 sts).

Row 4: (P6, m1) 4 times (28 sts).

Row 5: M1, k28, m1 (30 sts).

Row 6: (P7, m1) 4 times, p2 (34 sts).

Continue straight for 5 rows.

Row 12: M1, p34, m1 (36 sts).

Continue straight in St st for 27 rows depending on shape of car.

Row 40: P2tog, p32, p2tog (34 sts).

Row 41: K.

Row 42: (P2tog, p6) 4 times, p2 (30 sts)

Row 43: K2tog, k26, k2tog (28 sts).

Row 44: (P2tog, p5) 4 times (24 sts).

Row 45: K2tog, k20, k2tog (22 sts).

Row 46: (P1, p2tog) 6 times, p4 (16 sts).

Row 47: K2tog, k12, k2tog (14 sts).

Now continue with tail section, working from ** on page 116

Make up as for the toy-free snake (see opposite), but when you come to the central part of the snake's body, position a toy car on the knitting and sew the body around it.

Tina Tremble

MATERIALS

- 3.25 mm (US 3) and 5 mm (US 8) needles
- Black DK (sport) yarn
- Oddments of orange and dark green DK (sport) yarn
- Oddments of 9 other colours for leg warmers and hat
- 8 pipe cleaners
- 2 glass beads for eyes
- Tapestry or yarn needle and long needle or bodkin
- Scissors, sewing needle and black thread
- Toy stuffing (Polyfill)

The procecure

BODY (MAKE 1)

Using 2 strands of black yarn and 3.25 mm (US 3) needles, CO 5 sts.

Rows 1, 3 and 5: K.

Row 2: P2, m1, p1 m1, p1, m1, p1 (8 sts).

Row 4: P2, m1, p2, m1, p2, m1, p2, m1 (12 sts).

Row 6: P2, (m1, p2) 3 times, p2, m1, p2 (16 sts).

Row 7: K2, m1, k8, m1, k6 (18 sts).

Row 8: P2, m1, p5, m1, p4, m1, p5, m1, p2 (22 sts).

Row 9: K5, m1, k11, m1, k6 (24 sts).

Row 10: P3, (p6, m1) 3 times, m1, p3 (28 sts).

Row 11 and all alt rows: Knit.

Row 12: P3, (m1, p7) 3 times, m1, p4 (32 sts).

Row 14: P4, (m1, p8) 3 times, m1 p4 (36 sts).

Row 16: P9, m1, p18, m1, p9 (38 sts).

Now start decreasing:

Row 18: P9, p2tog, p17, p2tog, p8 (36 sts).

Row 20: P4, (p2tog, p7) 3 times, p2tog, p3 (32 sts).

Row 22: P7, p2tog, p14, p2tog, p7 (30 sts).

Row 24: P7, p2tog, p13, p2tog, p6 (28 sts).

Row 26: P6, p2tog, p12, p2tog, p6 (26 sts).

Row 28: P6, p2tog, p11, p2tog, p5 (24 sts).

Row 29: Break yarn and thread through rem sts.

HEAD

Usng 2 strands of black yarn and 3.25 mm (US 3) needles, CO 5 sts.

Row 1: K5.

Row 2: M1, p2, m1, p2, m1, p1 (8 sts).

Row 3: K8.

Row 4: P1, (m1, p2) 3 times, m1, p1 (12 sts).

Row 5: K12.

Row 6: P1, m1, p3, (m1, p2) 2 times, m1, p3, m1, p1 (17 sts).

Row 7: K4, m1, k9, m1, k4 (19 sts).

Row 8: P2, (m1, p5) 3 times, m1, p1, m1, p1 (24 sts).

Row 9 and every alt row: Knit.

Row 10: P2, (m1, p4) 5 times, m1, p2 (30 sts).

Row 12: P3, m1, p8, m1, p7, m1, p8, m1, p4 (34 sts).

Row 14: P8, m1, p17, m1, p9 (36 sts).

Row 15: K.

Now start decreasing.

Row 16: P8, p2tog, p16, p2tog, p8 (34 sts).

Row 18: P3, p2tog, p7, p2tog, p6, p2tog, p7, p2tog, p3 (30 sts).

Row 20: P3, p2tog, p6, p2tog, p5, p2tog, p6, p2tog, p2 (26 sts).

Row 22: P6, p2tog, p11, p2tog, p5 (24 sts).

Break yarn and thread through rem sts to close. To make up, stuff body and head with stuffing, stitch up, then stitch together. Using black thread and sewing needle, attach two beads for eyes.

LEGS (MAKE 4)

Using 1 strand of black yarn and 3.25 mm (US 3) needles, CO 4 sts. Knit every row until leg measures 36 cm (14 in). Bind off. This makes two of Tina's eight legs. Take 2 pipe cleaners and twist one end of each together to form a longer length and stitch sewing around them. Curl pipe cleaners at free ends to form feet. Repeat 3 more times until you have 4 long covered lengths. Attach at middle to bottom of body along seam.

LEG WARMERS (MAKE 8)

These are good for using up all those scraps of yarn as you will only need a small amount. Change colour as many times as you like to create stripes.

Using 1 strand of DK (sport) yarn and UK 3.25 mm (US 3) needles, CO 8 sts.

Work in St st, starting with a knit row, until you have 20 rows or piece measures 5.5 cm (2 in). Bind off and sew up sides. Put on Tina's legs, they should hold in place.

SCARF

Using 1 strand of blue yarn and 3.25 mm (US 3) needles, CO 6 sts.

Row 1: K with blue.

Row 2-3: K with orange.

Knit every row, changing colour every other row until the scarf measures 44 cm (17 in).

Bind off.

Sew in ends and make small tassels at either end.

HAT

Using 2 strands of purple yarn and 3.25 mm (US 3) needles, CO 30 sts.

Work in St st decreasing 2 sts at each edge every other row until 8 sts remain.

Next row: (K2tog) 4 times. Break yarn and pick up last 4 sts with the yarn and draw through. Sew up the side seam.

Place on Tina's head and fix in place with a few small stitches.

PUMPKIN

Using 2 strands of orange yarn and 5 mm (US 8) needles, CO 46 sts.

Row 1: K.

Row 2: P, (k, p) rep to end.

These 2 rows form pattern. Continue until piece measures 20 cm (8 in). Break yarn and thread through rem sts; pull tight. Use yarn to stitch up side seam, stuffing as you go. To create pumpkin shape use long needle to insert yarn through centre of ball to make indent.

PUMPKIN STALK

Using single strand of green yarn and 5 mm (US 8) needles, CO 6 sts.

Row 1: K.

Row 2: P2tog, p3, p2tog (4 sts).

Continue in St st until stalk is appropriate length or 2.5 cm (1 in).

Bind off; fix to the indent of your pumpkin.

The Snails

MATERIALS

- 5 mm (US 8) needles
- DK (sport) yarn in grey, white, red and black
- Yarn oddments for pompoms
- Card or pompom template (see page 124)
- Tapestry or yarn needle
- Scissors
- Toy stuffing (Polyfill)

The procedure

SNAIL BODY

Using 2 strands of grey yarn, CO 5 sts.

Work 3 rows St st beginning with a K row.

Row 4: P1, m1, p to end of row.

Row 5: K6 sts.

Row 6: P1, m1, p to end (7 sts).

Work 3 rows St st.

Row 10: P1, m1, p5, m1, p1 (9 sts).

Work 3 rows St st.

Row 14: P1, m1, (p3, m1) 2 times, p2 (12 sts).

Row 15: K.

Row 16: P3, m1, p6, m1, p3 (14 sts).

Work St st for 32 rows.

Next row: (P2tog) 7 times.

Break yarn and using needle, thread last 7 sts together. Sew up side seam, adding stuffing as you go. Create body shape by working additional stitches with sewing needle as you make up. To tilt head, bend thicker end back and stitch to body.

HORNS

Take a 20 cm (8 in) length of grey yarn. Twist the yarn until it bends in the centre. Allow this to twist up and then repeat so your twisted yarn is 4 strands thick. Make another horn like this and sew to the back of your snail's head.

TALL ROUND HOUSE

Using 2 strands of white yarn, CO 30 sts.

Row 1: K.

Row 2: P13 in W (white), p4 in B (black), p13 in W.

Keeping 4 central sts in black for the door, work 6 rows St st.

Row 9: P7, p2tog, p13, p2tog, p6 (28 sts).

Work 5 rows St st.

Row 15: P3, (p2tog, p5) 3 times, p2tog, p2 (24 sts).

Row 16: K8 in W, k2 in B, k4 in W, k2 B, k8 W.

Row 17: P8 in W, p2 in B, p4 in W, p2 B, p8 W.

Work 2 rows St st in W.

Row 20: P5, p2tog, p10, p2tog, p5 (22 sts).

7 rows St st.

Bind off.

For the shorter, wider house, work as for the tall house, but begin by casting on 52 sts. Work 3 windows across.

BASE OF TALL ROUND HOUSE

Using 2 strands of white yarn, CO 4.

Row 1 and all alt rows: K.

Row 2: M1, p4, m1 (6 sts).

Row 4: M1, p3, m1, p3, m1 (9 sts).

Row 6: (M1, p3) 3 times (12 sts).

Row 8: M1, p12, m1 (14 sts).

Work 3 rows St st then reverse shaping until 4 sts remain.

Bind off last 4 sts.

Sew the base to the house with white yarn.

ROOF OF TALL ROUND HOUSE

Using 2 strands of red yarn, CO 30 sts.

Work in St st dec 2 sts at each edge every other row until 8 sts remain.

Next row: (K2tog) 4 times. Break yarn and pick up last 4 sts with the yarn and draw through. This will form the cone for your roof.

To make the chimney, CO 6 sts in 2 strands of red yarn.

Row 1: K.

Row 2: P2tog, p3, p2tog (4 sts).

Continue in St st until chimney is appropriate length or 2.5 cm (1 in).

Bind off and fix to roof.

For roof of shorter house, CO 52 sts, then follow pattern.

CHURCH AND TOWER

Using 2 strands of white yarn, CO 20 sts.

Row 1: K.

Row 2: P8 in W, p4 in B, p8 in W.

Keeping 4 central sts in black for the door, work 4 rows St st.

Work 2 rows St st in white.

Next row: K8, m1 in W, k2 in B, k8, m1 in W.

Next row: P10 in W, p2 in B, p10 in W.

Work 2 rows St st in white.

Next row: K10 sts in W, k2 in B, k10 in W.

Next row: P10 in W, p2 in B, p10 in W.

Work another 14 rows St st in white.

Bind off and sew up back seam.

To make base for tower, CO 4 in white. Increase 2 sts each row until there are 8 sts, then reverse the shaping until there are 4 sts again. Cast off and sew to base of tower.

Make the roof as for the Tall Roundhouse.

NAVE

Using 2 strands of white yarn and 5 mm (US 8) needles, CO 12 sts.

Work St st for 32 rows.

Bind off. Fold in half and sew seams up the sides.

To make nave roof, using 2 strands of red yarn, CO 20 sts.

Work 12 rows in garter st. Bind off. Fold in half, position on top of nave and sew into place.

Sew nave to tower.

MAKING UP THE HOUSES

Sew up your buildings down the back using the same colour yarn, stuffing as you go. You could use heavier stuffing material, such as old tights or foam chips, at the base of your houses, to make sure that they stand upright.

POMPOMS

Make a template by drawing 2 circles on card each 13 cm (5 in) in diameter (see template on page 124). Cut out. Make 5 cm (2 in) diameter holes in the centres, so they look like 2 large letter Os. Place these together and wind your snail's choice of coloured yarn around the template. Change colour as many times as you like until you the hole in the centre starts to disappear. Now be bold and cut the yarn around the outside. The scissors can go into the space between the 2 template pieces. Take a length of yarn and wrap it tightly around the centre of the yarn in between the two cards, knotting tight to secure it. Remove the cards and fluff up your pompom. Make 1 for each snail.

Honey Bee Mine

MATERIALS

- 3.5 mm (US 4) needles
- Offcuts of DK yarn in yellow, black and white for the bee
- DK yarn in red for heart
- 1 pair of small googly eyes
- Stitch holder or safety pin
- Tapestry or yarn needle
- Scissors
- Toy stuffing (Polyfill)

The procedure

BEE BODY (MAKE 1)

Using black yarn, CO 10 sts.

Row 1: Knit (10 sts).

Row 2: M1, p10, m1 (12 sts).

Row 3: K12.

Row 4: *K2, m1* rep to end (18 sts).

Rows 5-6: Continuing in stocking stitch, change to yellow for 2 rows.

Rows 7-8: Make 2 rows in black.

Rows 9-10: Make 2 rows in yellow.

Rows 11-12: Make 2 rows in black.

Rows 13-15: Make 3 rows in yellow.

Row 16: K2tog, p to last 2 sts and ktog.

Row 17: K (16 sts).

Row 18: *P2, p2tog* rep to end (10 sts).

Row 19: K 10.

Bind off.

WINGS (MAKE 2)

Using white yarn, CO 4 sts.

Knit 2 rows In garter stitch.

Row 3: M1, k4 (5 sts).

Row 4: K5.

Row 5: M1, k5 (6 sts).

Row 6: K6.

Row 7: K2tog, k4 (5 sts).

Row 8: K5.

Row 9: K2tog, k3 (4 sts).

Row 10: K4.

Bind off.

Make another wing reversing shaping by making increases and decreases at the end of the row.

MAKING UP THE BEE

To make up, sew the sides of the stripy bee together, stuffing as you go. Attach the wings on either side of the bee's yellow head section.

HEART (MAKE 2)

Using red yarn, CO 2 sts.

Row 1: K1, m1, k1 (3 sts).

Row 2: P3.

Row 3: M1, k3, m1 (5 sts).

Row 4 and every alt row: P.

Row 5: M1, k5, m1 (7 sts).

Row 7: M1, k7, m1 (9 sts).

Row 9: M1, k9, m1 (11 sts).

Row 11: M1, k11, m1 (13 sts).

Row 13: M1, k13, m1 (15 sts).

Row 15: K2tog, k11, k2tog (13 sts).

Row 16: P13.

Row 17: K2tog, k5. Turn, leaving remaining 6 sts on a stitch holder.

Row 18: P6.

Row 19: K2tog, k2, k2tog (4 sts).

Row 20: P4.

Row 21: Bind off.

Rejoin yarn to remaining 6 sts and reverse shaping on the other side.

Next row: P6.

Next row: K2tog, k2, k2tog (4 sts).

Next row: P4.

Next row: Bind off.

Make another heart shape and sew both together, stuffing as you go.

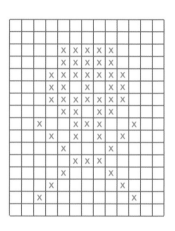

Pirate Thing's eye
patch (see page 107)

Templates

Pirate Thing's Jolly
Roger chart
(page 107)

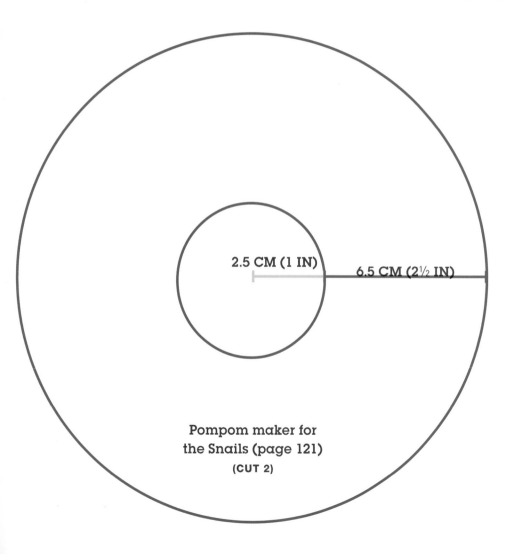

2.5 CM (1 IN)

6.5 CM (2½ IN)

Pompom maker for
the Snails (page 121)
(CUT 2)

Tongue for Snakes in
the City (page 116)

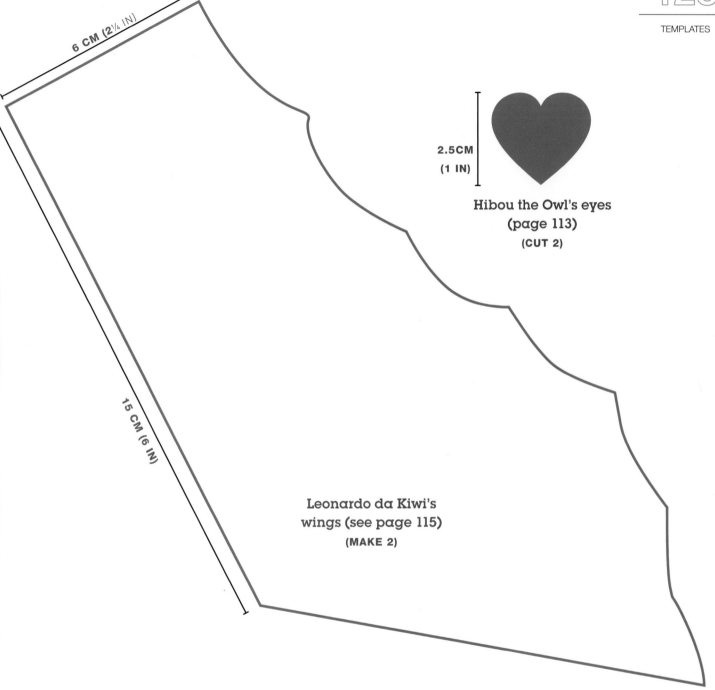

6 CM (2¼ IN)

15 CM (6 IN)

2.5CM
(1 IN)

Hibou the Owl's eyes
(page 113)
(CUT 2)

**Leonardo da Kiwi's
wings (see page 115)**
(MAKE 2)

Index

The author would like to thank...

My mum and sisters Azucena, Dalia, Rosi and Yoly for opening my eyes to knitting and handmade things. Amanda Barnsley for her advice and for always being so enthusiastic about my work. Victoria Jane Siddle for spotting the publishing opportunity. Judith and Jenny for making the book happen. My family, the Spanish and the English. My friends, and Mariajo especially always there. And finally and a million times to my Benji for giving me wings. Love to all.

Fil Rouge Press would like to thank...

Jean-Philippe Woodland; Jennifer Latham; Elizabeth Healey; Katy Bevan; Apiary Studios.; Percy Ingle.